Poems and Haiku

Nicholas K F Matte

Samkhya Publishing

Samkhya Publishing
& 2020 Nicholas K F Matte

All rights reserved
No part of this work covered by the copyrights herein, may be reproduced in any form or by any means, graphic, electronic, or mechanical. Without the prior written permission of the publisher.

National Library Archives of Canada
Cataloguing in Publishing Data.
Matte, Nicholas K F
Poems and Haiku
2020
ISBN: 978-1-9991955-2-6

Contents

Large Buddha Statues and Daibutsu Poems

1 Fourth Bamiyan Buddha
4 Kamakura Buddha
6 Tian Tan Buddha
8 Nihon-ji Buddha
9 Leshan Giant Buddha
11 Hussain Sagar Buddha
12 Spring Time Buddha

Haiku for Notable Persons

13 Miyamoto Musashi
14 Takuan Soho
15 Ikkyu Sojun
16 Eisai
17 Bodhidharma
18 Hui-Neng
19 Mahakashyapa

Haiku

20 Fishing haiku
21 Morning Haiku
22 Sky Orange...
23 The Mountain...
24 The Flowers...

25 Kaihogyo monk
26 Red Tailed Hawk...
27 Lovely trees...
28 Busy fish Market
29 Fast Fiery Star
30 Chess...
31 Million Dollar Koi
32 In a Cloudless Sky
33 A Stone Holds Firm There

Poems

34 A Zalabian and his Horse in Wadi Rum
36 The Pride of Gujarat
37 An Egyptian Caracal
38 A Poem for the River Po
39 The Temple of Dove
40 Short Poem for Li Po
41 Ahmose and Kuleg winning the Race of the Harvest Horse Race
43 The House of Avtinas
44 A Glimpse at Wat Pho
  The Guardians of Wat Pho
45 The Eagle-hunters of Mongolia
46 The Berbers
47 In Caesarea
48 Short Poem for Dave Holland
49 Poem for Honen
51 The Prayer to Fudo Myoo
52 Poem for the Ainu
54 The Panthera Leo
56 Salaman at the Ghats

Large Buddha Statue
and
Daibutsu Poems

The 4th Bamiyan Buddha

Before Lord Christ by a millennium
Silk was worn in ancient Egypt
By the routes Sino Idiom
This brilliance was wrought and shipped

Later the great Mandarin grasp
Acquired Dayuan steed
Before the Farghana one did gasp
The Horses of Heavenly Breed

Oc Eo the beauty Vietnam
Gold was found on site
Minted and brought to the calm
Of this wonder of day and night

Trade from Silla, Baekje and Gorgurgeo
Vital ginseng for Romulus wear
To Cheju, Korean straight, fantastic clio
Came heat from Arabian lair

Women of the Senator's heart
Loved their reflected radiance
Edicts dispensed but failed to part
The beauties from decadent adience

Byzantium Nestorians stole protein
From China eggs were taken
Thrace in the North began to lean
On the trade it did awaken

Near Tian Shan, Yuezhin, Bactrian
Where flows the Oxus Amo
The Hindu Kush, the Pamir
Came Buddhist wealth to sow

In Bamyan were built the great
Statues that once stood so grand
A new one was found reclining late
Within Nirvana's hand

Xuan Zang, Hiuen Tsang many a word
Was a Mahayana scholar
Sanskrit in wealth these words he heard
In a dream to travel farther

Turpan the Flaming Mountains rose
Before his very eyes
The king of these hills whom he now knows
Gave him a hand, no lies

In Afghanistan he stood in awe
Before the statues of might
Symbol of footprint, symbol of umbrella
Were extrapolated without a fight

A 300 foot reclining Buddha of peace
Zang witnessed upon his stay
1000 legs, gold gilt lease
A wonder from May to May

Back to China he returned fit
To teach his students many
A statue holds true by fires lit
Great Goose Pagoda hosts plenty

I do believe the moment near prime
For this long sought astonishing wonder
Fourth Buddha of Bamiyan in time
Will surface with overwhelming thunder

Kamakura Buddha
(written before reading Kipling's poem, with one correction made)

Rescuer of Souls
Bronze, once wood, a statue
Around the ears, some gold

Graffiti wrought by pen
Many a prayer within
This like a fox's den

Tsunami of Meio
Destroyed the outer abode
Waves came high and crashing
In crescent mode

Still it stood in reverence
Many a storm it survived
Wonderful to stand before it
And take in the bounty derived

Wonderful the blessed Daibutsu
Statue for Billions of lives
Wonderful the blessed Daibutsu
Wonderful for one who strives

Amitabha
(written after reading Kipling's poem)

Enhancer of Souls
Bronze, once leafed gold
There for all to see
Everyone, young and old

Tibetan Mara would once and for all fold
Beneath this statue's might
Holy place of pilgrimage trode
Among the stars of night

Tian Tan Buddha

In the South China Sea
Lantau Island was fitted to be
Tian Tan Shakyamuni
Sits in the land of the Yangtze

Like the Altar of Heaven beyond
Of which all are immensely fond
The ancient wisdom here dawned
The base of intellect, statue brawned

Offering of the six Gods
The perfection of generosity one greatly applauds
Perfection of morality, wisdom, patience, meditation and zeal one greatly nods
Enlightenment impossible sans these qualities and lauds

Flowers, lamp, fruit, incense, ointment, and music offered
To think of the melodies in the air from the Deva's coffer
Inspiring the multitudes to prosper
In wonderful Chan beauty to heal the suffered

The bronze right hand is raised
Removing all affliction blazed
Like a flame leaving one amazed
The devoted are thus praised

The left hand rests upon his lap
Generosity, like a tree's sap
Goodness does now awaken and tap
Like the ignition from a Zen clap

The Halls of the Universe and Merit
Of Remembrance, what spirit
Gautama's remains are there to cherish
Prayers rise high and inherit

Forged of bronze and shinning gold
There for the young and old
Tian Tan Buddha
An experience manifold

Nihon-ji Daibutsu

On the slopes of Nokogiri
Made sacred by the priest Guden
Stands the Daibutsu of Nyorai
Healer of all through zen

Much destruction it has seen
Earthquake, riots, fire
But always to be rebuilt
To perfection from the dire

Now a Soto temple
India sent as a gift
A sapling of his Bodhi Tree
Spirits at once do lift

Leshan Giant Buddha

From a cliff of red sandstone
Was built during the Tang dynasty
Facing Mount Emei on it's own
Min and Dadu confluency

In a baffling rage
Hai Tong's sight himself gouged
Hoping the Buddha would mage
The fast waters being bouged

Maitreya, seated, hands on knees
Through deep conquering meditation
From Tusita Heaven he has achieved
Mirth and woe cessation

He will attain bodhi in seven days
Under the Mesua Ferrea tree
Compassionate his intelligent gaze
Leading all to be free

Eighty-eight cubits tall will he be
And for eighty-eight thousand years he will walk
Showing our world the wonderful key
Healing our world which was turned distraught

The statue of Leshan watches careful
The rivers below
The boats are safe now
Onward sailing they go

Hussain Sagar Buddha

Inspired by Bartholdi and Eiffel
Witnessed by one in awe
Hussain Sagar Buddha does tell
The wisdom of Shakyamuni law

The sufi saint of Galkonda
Filled the heart shaped lake
Friends with Shahi Shah
Many responsibilities did he take

A piece of solid white granite was found
To be worked upon by hundreds of labourers
Through many moon revolutions round
Did they chisel in mantric murmurs

The tallest monolithic Buddha
In this entire world
Consecrated by the Dalai Lama
Hope and prayer unfurled

Spring Time Buddha

Always Tranquil Light
The All of Vairocana
Primordial being teacher
Adi-Buddha Hosanna

In Fudoshan scenic area
Within earshot of the Bell of Good Luck
Stands the Buddha of Impermanence
Our souls are at once struck

Second tallest statue in the world
Stands above a monastery of peace
Copper cast on a lotus base
Our bounties of Good increase

Named after the nearby spring
Water of which can cure
The pilgrimage sets the very soul
In emancipative freedom pure

At the top of Dragon Head Peak
The bell rings aloud
Lifting our thoughts heavenwards
Lifting ignorance like a shroud

Haiku For Notable Persons

Miyamoto Musashi

Two swords in his hands
Movement flowing like a wave
Brilliant in all realms

Takuan Soho

Sword wielding Buddhist
Monk of exquisite insight
Radish on a plate

Ikkyu Sojun

Walking a dirt road
The thud of a walking stick
Madness in his eyes

Eisai

Bringing Chinese seeds
Of mind and also of tea
His first temple built

Bodhidharma

Long did he travel
Bringing true enlightenment
Wall gazer in cave

Hui-Neng

Chopping wood for sale
The diamond sutra he heard
Open Buddha mind

Mahakashyapa

Udunbara bloom
Buddha teaching his sangha
One smiles at the back

Haiku

Fishing Haiku

Fish within the net
Waves above are not too strict
Appetites are whet

Morning Haiku

Sun's rays healing some
Standing in the morning's light
Below a dog barks

Sky orange...

Sky orange colour
Mars to show it's light tonight
A bat is circling

The mountain...

The mountain stands firm
Shadowing the countryside
Sun still rising high

The flowers...

The flowers in bloom
In the garden by the well
Welcome bees and flies

Kaihogyo monk...

Kaihogyo monk
Circling on the mountain paths
No viper will strike

Red tailed hawk...

Red tailed hawk circling
Chased by pigeons and ravens
Tennis on the set

Lovely trees...

Lovely trees swaying
By the lake in the valley
Now soon to come rain

Busy fish market

Busy fish market
The sight of cod, shrimp, eel
A tobacco cloud

Fast fiery star

Fast fiery star
Tears a cloud in the night sky
Eyes look heavenwards

Chess...

Chess pieces placed there
Beneath the heat of the day
New York City park

Million dollar koi

Million dollar koi
Nippon flag on it's head
Happy customer

In a cloudless sky

In a cloudless sky
The whippoorwill flies to her
Beneath the moon, love

A stone holds firm there

A stone holds firm there
In a garden far beyond
Find it, it will smile

Poems

A Zalabian and his Horse in Wadi Rum

From the village beyond the dunes
Comes a man in humble guise
But nodding his head in discontentment
Nodding to counter heard lies

Away from the killing stress
Of the troubles back and away
It's in a soulful spirit
He truly wishes to stay

Dressed in a long white tunic
Keffiyeh of red and white
Sandals, rings, and necklace
He focuses on the light

He stops and calls surrender
To his steed, an Arabian black
Now waiting with impatience
Enthusiasm no longer in lack

Over and down the iron-red dune
Comes galloping his horse Sadiq
Much elegance to behold
This mount of the desert sheik

The bedouin's heart is fully blessed
By the site of this friend approaching
Tears well up, he touches his chin
Amazed at this vision in motion

Elegance and strength
Bewildering the mind
Cleverness and beauty
From front to hind

With arms outstretched the Zalabian catches
This equine perfection beast
About the neck, they greet, happy
In the desert of the East

They run a bit, in the "Roman Valley"
Energized in their unity
He talks kind words of stately joy
Fortifying their immunity

He swings up Sadiq, onto his back
And pets his mane and shoulders
Whispering in his ear, they now tear
Across Rum towards many beholders

The Pride of Gujarat

On the Arabian Sea coast
Friend of the Maldharis
Gir and Girnam host
The avatar of Vishnu Is

An Egyptian Caracal

An Egyptian Caracal comes running in
Into the palace before the Queen
The Nile has flooded now
The land where she had once been

Years before on a hunt for mice
And searching for a mate
By the papyrus along the shore
Far from the sandstone gate

First a growl and then a purr
She alights to a table top
The Queen pets her friend's ears
Mutual love nothing can stop

Amon Ra now lowers in the sky
The Earth revolving in turn
Content before a plate of fish
Whims no longer churn

A Poem for the River Po

Bubbling forth
From a pristine spring
Cottian Alps
Mount Viso brings

The Bottomless Po
According to etymology
Foundation to the Greek
Sanskrit depth of psychology

Was it where Phaethon
In forest form
Brought tears of amber
Aft the lightning storm

And could it of been Eridamas
Much sung by poets of yore
River in the sky
Greek mythology is sure

Leonardo Da Vinci
Opened his mind
To build canals
In Milan you'll find

But at the end of the Val Padana
Cherished by the Roman mass
Eels are found in abundance
For a meal and notes of brass

The Temple of Dove
(Fictional Chan Buddhist Temple)

Sweeping Buddha
Of ancient Chan
Sweeping Buddha
Of all the land

Speaking with birds
Up high in the trees
Eyeing the cats
Mellow in the breeze

Sweeping the steps
Of the Temple of Dove
Sweeping the dust
(Of) The mind, the tongue

Clearing the worms
By hand, one by one
He's clearing the paths
On which dirt once clung

Short poem for Li Po

Li Po, what imagination
A sip for the Moon
The hand doth point
To this companion boon

A traveller in life
Breathing the vital inspiring air
Of life on the go
Always heading somewhere

Li Po, a sip for the Moon
Another poem for all
Make us smile in wonderment
Your words! Our hearts will never fall

Ahmose and Kuleg winning the Race of
the Harvest Horse Race

On the hieroglyph walls
Of Ancient Egypt's tombs
The steeds are depicted
In epic warring feuds

From Arabia they came
Not God's of their pantheon
But embraced by the Pharaohs
For their wealth of fiery brawn

A whistle is heard
And Ahmose is in awe
When directly to him comes galloping
This wildness of unsurpassed joie

"Kalug I shall call you
Horse of steadfast speed
Our legend will be set
On beautiful papyrus reed"

For practice-course they ride around
The town in hoof beating haste
Leaving all in a cloud of dust
Like this in ferocious pace

After riding they spend their time
In the dunes of the ensuing desert
Watching dusk in contemplation
The sky in extraordinary concert

Race day is upon them in the valley beyond
Dozens of racers are there
Horses heaving in dramatic display
In anticipation they cannot bare

A horn is blown and ululation is sounded
The mounts speed on their way
Beautiful women cheer riders and steeds
Some begin to pray

Across much desert they travel in clusters
Like stars in a brilliant night
But each on their own working hard to arrive first
To the finish-line way out of sight

The heat of the Sun comes blaring down
On the participants as they approach
The crowds again, hands up in air
The men begin to coach

It's Ahmose and Kuleg who are first at the line
Tears of wonder swell
Their friendship is applauded, highest and praised
Ambition begins to tell

The House of Avtinas

Bearers of the sacred smoke
Women of secret thought
Like ancient music baroque
Mixture, excellence well wrought
K---. throws in the sea-shells
L---. saffron, salt and gums
P---. the maalah ashan, that keeps the
cloud straight at all sums
Filling Solomon's Temple
With the raising of faithful prayer
The women, no perfume, cheerful
Smile and chat, when this, they prepare

A Glimpse at Wat Pho

Rama III in '32
Built the "Lovely Eyes"
Which closed in the past
Cessation of truth and lies (Samsara)

The Guardians of Wat Pho

As ballast for a ship
The protectors of the gate
Were brought Haiwai (over seas)
To their righteous fate

To guard the doors of Pho
Wat Pho on Temple grounds
Some Euro. In design
All wonderful, ruthless hounds

Straight in their demeanors
Weapons all in hand
The guardians of the way
Tao for ever grand

The Eagle Hunters Of Mongolia

The eaglet is taken from the nest
Of the golden bird of truth
Raised and kept for four years best
This creature is pride in sooth

Three riders atop a hillock look
Across the dust laden valley
Dressed ornately like from a book
Of brilliance from start to finale

A fox is spotted in the distance
Hearts pounding at the apex
The first asserts his existence
Releasing in a state of Rex

The eagle makes a good attempt
The fox is wounded shortly
The second rider yells to tempt
His bird to attack thwartly

But it's the third hunter who claims the kill
His bird deals the final blow
He feeds his eagle down the hill
With fox's foot and toe

He will now wear, the felled beast's pelt
Proudly, in recognition
As a prize, hanging, from his belt
Claiming the hunt's fruition

The Berbers

North African guard
Expansive in mass
Best horsemen of bard
No singing without class

Phoenician colonies
Within their lands
Brought Tyrian glories
Of purple dyed hands

In the days of Carthage
Dido was the Queen
Lady of the womb
Of the world she must of been

They gave to her the land
By strips of an ox's hide
Byrsa was established
Embryo of future pride

Hiarbus the chieftain
Relished in his design
But, alas Dido's want
Was finalized with a sigh

Rustic they were all
In Mediterranean space
Not quite as elegant
As the Pharaoh's of Lybian grace

In Caesarea

In Caesarea
Where lights are fires in the periphery
In Caesarea
Where a Roman aqueduct leads to the ancient rubbled city
In Caesarea
Where a coin was found in sand not deep
In Caerarea
Where wild dogs run manic, but never leap
In Caesarea
Where the sea is refreshing, brilliantly cold
In Caesarea
Where cliffs are a stage for the many so bold
In Caesarea
Where fishermen catch bream from below the waves
In Caesarea
Where the air heals, our souls it saves
In Caesarea
Where the Sun blares down in wondrous tones
In Caesarea
Where the Moon, hums, whispers, atones
In Caesarea

Short poem for Dave Holland

Dave Holland's fingers flip through a book
Note for note his superb music gives us a look
At this steadfast brilliant genius

He is one in this great swelling sound
Double bass in hand
Euphony found
Double bass in hand
Smiles abound

Poem for Honen

Namesake with Amida's Seichen
Taught on the cliffs of Mount Hiei
The 7th Patriarch of Jodo-Shu
Lifts our souls inconceivably high

The heart of his devotion
Tokikuni's wishes burn ignorance
Upon his deathbed were expressed
A future of prayer and deliverance

After relishing Shandao Zendo
Chion-in was constructed
Site where he taught the many
Sanmon Gate, here he instructed

Once exiled to Sanuki
Healed prostitutes and fishermen
Emperor Go-Toba gave a criminal's name
He returned with the winter's wren

In the Higashiyama Mountains in Kyoto
One can hear a thunderous bell
Seventeen men it takes
To play it's music well

Much simpler are the ways of Nianfo
Holding the Saint's name in trust
Repetition and devotion
For when we return to dust

The Prayer to Fudo Myoo

Greatest God Fudo
Sword cutting through illusion
Reigning over evil passions
He is the Immovable One
---------   ---------   ---------
Forlorn soul approaches now
Statue by the path
Prayer and emancipation, a bow
Reborn with righteous wrath

With the newly found wisdom
This soul continues on
A journey of blessed rhythm
From night into the dawn

Poem for the Ainu

Of blood with the people of Tibet
And the Andaman Islands I'm told
The Ainu of Japan, strong, heavy set
Beautiful culture, caring, intelligent, bold

In history came the Children of the Sun
For which my heart bleeds
Hokkaido, Sakhalin, and Kuril won
The Ainu people's indomitable deeds

The Ainu are hunters by design
With their dogs they caught their prey
In the winter when the mountains hide
The Ezo deer within the brae

For love a man ate half a bowl of rice
Then gave it to his be-loved
If she ate and thought him nice
Prayers were sent above

Kamuy, Great God of the Bear
Was praised in exuberant display
A celebration conducted there
By the village chief of the day

After many years set alone
The Ainu have received their right
The bounty of this world will be shown
To this people of ancient might

The Panthera Leo

Emblem of great ancient Persia
The roars once heard in the night
Two pillars of wisdom and of courage
Were raised to protect the right

Egypt's Sekhmet, what righteous role
To guard against famine and disease
The people were safe, hearts whole
Their fears were put at ease

The Greeks would hunt this beast for sport
In show of might, of strength
And Xerxes' camels were attacked left mort
Between Nestus' and Achelous' length

Surviving almost to this day
The Barbary lion did prowl
Algeria, Morocco, it did pray
Wild boar, red deer, full jowl

The Romans captured these fiery beasts
To set their arenas for show
Celebrating the days of feasts
The populous were sure to go

To the Hindu the Mahabharata does speak
Of Narasimha, man-lion of fierce karma
Avatar of Vishnu, apex, peek
Of the law which restores the Dharma

Tibet has the snow lion as it's symbol
Pure fearlessness and joy
Shinning forth like a brilliant crystal
Nothing can destroy

His first speech at Sarnath Deer Park
Was absolute knowledge, wisdom
The "Lion's Roar" did wonderfully spark
All minds to ultimate rhythm

Salaman at the Ghats

Salaman makes his way to the ghats in Varanasi.
Holding a silver cup he found in town.
The scent of burning wood is in the air from
another ghat near, rising from the several
cremation pyres there. 88 ghats there are at that
blessed city.
Putting his palms together he stabilizes himself.
Then walks down to the bottom steps.
He turns around, lights a candle and chants.
OM ARAPACANA DHIH
(perfection of wisdom and learning)

Turning back toward the rising sun to the east,
it's light-force healing his eyes, strengthening
his demeanor, in the explosive fortitude of the
morning sky.

He then steps down into the water, sand soft
and warm beneath his feet.

With his cup, he pours The Great Ganga's life-
stream over his head, rinses his mouth, spitting
happily, washing his body, communing with the
world.

Then, smiling, seeing a beautiful woman, he
whistles a tune. She laughs and waves. He
waves back.

Happy, he turns back to the morning sun.

Embracing all, he chants to Mother Earth.
 "Great Goddess of Life, Grant me the Serenity
of Peace and Joy, God Bless! God Bless!
OM MANI PADME HUM
OM MANI PADME HUM
(freedom from pain and giving of compassion)

A special thanks to my father Kempton Matte, my uncle Charles J LaBelle, my late mother Helene Ouimet, and Anton Luneau, Sue Zolmer, and all the rest of my family and friends. The Shepherds of Good Hope, The Salvation Army, The Ottawa Mission, La Maison Benoit Labre, The Old Brewery Mission, Accueil Bonneau, Welcome Mission Hall, La Maison du Pere, Causeway Work Center and the Ottawa Food Bank.

Thank you greatly.
NKFM

Nicholas K F Matte is a writer, musician, poet, living in Ottawa Ontario, Canada. He has a certificate in orchestra conducting from the University of Montreal. He has studied english literature and the history of cinema at McGill University. He is an avid classical, jazz, blues and rock guitarist and composer. He greatly enjoys the martial art of kendo and the sport of boxing.

samkhyapublishing@gmail.com

10% of purchase price goes to a local charity.

www.ingramcontent.com/pod-product-compliance
Lightning Source LLC
Chambersburg PA
CBHW020020050426
42450CB00005B/559